Learning SPARK

Analytics With Spark Framework

Tables of Contents

Introduction

Spark is a very useful framework for use in cloud computing. It is well known for how it speeds up the process of analytical processing. It is good for the writing of algorithms, and especially the ones to be used for machine learning. This book explores the various details on how Spark can be used for the purpose of processing analytics.

Chapter 1- Definition

Spark is an open-source framework for cluster computing. Its processing is done in-memory so that the speed of processing of analytic applications can be increased even up to 100 times faster as compared to the other technologies which are available in the market today. The development of the framework was done in the AMPLab at UC Berkeley. With this framework, the complexity involved in the interaction of data is greatly reduced. The speed of processing will also be greatly improved. The framework also has the effect of enhancing the effectiveness of mission critical applications with a very deep intelligence.

The framework is supported by different platforms, and this shows how flexible it is. The process of creating algorithms by use of Spark is very easy, and this makes it easy for its users to harness their insight from very complex data. In the year 2014, Spark was greatly expanded to a top level project. The expansion is still ongoing, and this shows how great the framework might be in the future. The framework is also well suitable for use with algorithms for machine learning. For you to use Spark, you are required to have a distributed storage system and a cluster manager. When it comes to cluster management, Spark will support Hadoop YARN, standalone or Apache Mesos. When it comes to a distributed storage, there is a wide variety of apps which can be interfaced with Spark.

Chapter 2- Spark Shell for Interactive Analysis

With the Spark shell, we can easily learn on how o use the API, and a powerful tool for an interactive analysis of data will be provided. The shell for Spark is available in Python or Scala. Note that Scala runs on the Java Virtual Machine (JVM).

Start the shell by navigating to the Spark directory, and then execute the following command:

For Scala users, execute the following command:

```
./bin/spark-shell
```

For Python users, run the following command:

```
./bin/pyspark
```

The primary abstraction for Spark is the RDD (Resilient Distributed Dataset) which is a distributed collection of items. To create RDDs, we can transform other RDDs or create them from the Hadoop InputFormats.

The README file contained in the root directory of Hadoop has some text. Let us try to make an RDD from this text by executing the following command:

```
>>> textFile = sc.textFile("README.md")
```

With RDDs, there are actions which return values, and there are transformations which will return pointers to other RDDs. Consider the actions given below:

```
>>> textFile.count()
```

The above command should give us the number of items which are contained in our RDD. Consider the next command given below:

```
>>> textFile.first()
```

The command given above will give us the first item which is contained in our RDD.

We now need to make use of a transformation. The filter transformation will be used for returning a new RDD having a subset of the items which are contained in the file. This is shown below:

```
>>> linesWithSpark = textFile.filter(lambda line: "Spark" in line)
```

The actions and the transformations can then be chained together as shown below:

```
>>> textFile.filter(lambda line: "Spark" in line).count()
```

The actions and transformations for RDD can be used for carrying out of more complex computations. Consider a scenario in which we need to find the line which is having the most words. This can be done by use of the command given below:

```
textFile.map(lambda line: len(line.split())).reduce(lambda x, y: x if (x > y) else y)
```

With the above line of code, the line will first be mapped to an integer value, and a new RDD will be created. The function "reduce" will then be called on the newly created RDD in that line, so that the largest line count is found. Consider the example given below:

```
def max(x, y):
...    if x > y:
...        return x
...    else:
...        return y
...
```

Once you have written the above, the following command should then be executed:

```
textFile.map(lambda line: len(line.split())).reduce(max)
```

MapReduce is one of the most command data flow patterns which are supported in Spark. This can easily be implemented in Spark as shown below:

wc = textFile.flatMap(lambda line: line.split()).map(lambda word: (word, 1)).reduceByKey(lambda x, y: x+y)

Note that in the above example, we have combined several transformations for the computation of the per word count in our file as an RDD of pairs of string and integer.

The "collect" action can be used for collection of the word count in the shell as shown below:

```
>>> wordCounts.collect()
```

Caching

With Spark, one can pull the data sets into a memory cache which is cluster-wide. This becomes very important in circumstances where the data has to be accessed repeatedly. A good example is when the algorithm that you are using is iterative. The data will not have to be fetched from the memory, which involves much overhead, but from the cache, which is faster and offers much less overhead. We need to demonstrate how caching can be done. Suppose that you want to mark a particular line to be cached, this can be done as follows:

```
>>> linesWithSpark.cache()
```

```
>>> linesWithSpark.count()
```

Note that you do not have to do caching on files which have very few lines. It is recommended that this should be done on files which have large data sets. Even if the data sets have been distributed across multiple nodes, the functions can be applied on them. The process can also be done interactively.

Writing Self-Contained Applications

Sometimes, you might need to use the Spark API so as to create self-contained applications. This can be done in Java, Scala, and Python.

The Python API, that is, PySpark, can be used for writing self-contained applications.

Scala

'We need to create a simple self-contained app with Scala. The code given below can be used for that purpose:

```
/* MyApp.scala */
import org.apache.spark.SparkContext._
import org.apache.spark.SparkContext
import org.apache.spark.SparkConf
object MyApp {
def main(args: Array[String]) {
val lFile = "YOUR_SPARK_HOME/README.md" // The file should be present in your system
val con = new SparkConf().setAppName("My Application")
val sc = new SparkContext(con)
val lData = sc.textFile(lFile, 2).cache()
val nAs = lData.filter(line => line.contains("x")).count()
val nBs = lData.filter(line => line.contains("y")).count()
println("Lines with x: %s, Lines with y: %s".format(nAs, nBs))
}
}
```

With the above example, the number of lines containing the letter "x" and the ones containing the letter "y" will be counted. These will be counted in the README file. The parameter "YOUR_SPARK_HOME" in the above code should be replaced with the location of Spark in your local system, otherwise, you will get an error. You also notice that we have initialized our own SparkContext, unlike what we have doing in the other examples. A repository on which Spark will depend on will also be created as shown below:


```
name := "My Project"
version := "1.0"
scalaVersion := "2.10.4"
lDependencies += "org.apache.spark" %% "spark-core" % "1.5.0"
```

We must lay the app according to the typical structure of the directory. It is after this that a JAR package containing the code for the application can be created, and then we will execute or run the program.

Java

The following code can be used for creation of a simple Spark application in the Java programming language:

```
/* MyApp.java */

import org.apache.spark.SparkConf;

import org.apache.spark.api.java.*;

import org.apache.spark.api.java.function.Function;

public class MyApp {

public static void main(String[] args) {

String lFile = " SPARK_HOME/README.md"; // This file should be available in your local system.

SparkConf con = new SparkConf().setAppName("My Application");

JavaSparkContext sc = new JavaSparkContext(con);

JavaRDD<String> lData = sc.textFile(logFile).cache();

long nAs = lData.filter(new Function<String, Boolean>() {

public Boolean call(String s) { return s.contains("x"); }

}).count();

long nBs = lData.filter(new Function<String, Boolean>() {

public Boolean call(String s) { return s.contains("y"); }
```

```
}).count();

System.out.println("Lines with x: " + nAs + ", lines with y: " +
nBs);
}
}
```

Similarly, the program given above will count the number of lines in the file README for the Spark which have the letters "x" and "y". The parameter "SPARK_HOME" has to be replaced with the location of the Spark in your system, otherwise, the program will not run. Note that we have also initialized a SparkContext, unlike in the other cases. For the purpose of building the application, a Maven "pon.xml" file should also be written and this will be used for listing Spark as a dependency. The artifacts for Spark are tagged with a version for Scala. This is shown below:

```
<project>
<groupId>me.program</groupId>
<artifactId>My-project</artifactId>
<modelVersion>4.0.0</modelVersion>
<name>My Project</name>
<packaging>jar</packaging>
<version>1.0</version>
<dependencies>
<dependency> <!-- Spark dependency -->
<groupId>org.apache.spark</groupId>
<artifactId>spark-core_2.10</artifactId>
<version>1.5.0</version>
</dependency>
</dependencies>
</project>
```

That is how it looks like.

Python

A simple Spark application can also be created by use of the Python API, that is, PyAPI. The following code can be used for creating the application "MyApp.py":

```
"""MyApp.py"""

from pyspark import SparkContext

lFile = " SPARK_HOME/README.md"   This file should be
available in your local system.

sc = SparkContext("local", "My App")

lData = sc.textFile(logFile).cache()

nAs = logData.filter(lambda s: 'x' in s).count()

nBs = logData.filter(lambda s: 'y' in s).count()

print("Lines with x: %i, lines with y: %i" % (nAs, nBs))
```

The above program will be used for counting the number of lines having the letters "x" and "y" in the file README of the Spark. Again, do not forget to replace the parameter "SPARK_HOME" with the location of the Spark installed on your system.

Consider the code given below, which shows how a simple job can be implemented in Java:

```java
/*** MyJob.java ***/

import spark.api.java.*;

import spark.api.java.function.Function;

public class MyJob {

public static void main(String[] args) {

String lFile = "/var/log/syslog"; // The file should be available
in your local system

JavaSparkContext sc = new JavaSparkContext("local", "My
Job",

"$ SPARK_HOME", new String[]{"target/my-project-
1.0.jar"});

JavaRDD<String> lData = sc.textFile(lFile).cache();

long nAs = lData.filter(new Function<String, Boolean>() {

public Boolean call(String s) { return s.contains("x"); }

}).count();

long numBs = logData.filter(new Function<String, Boolean>()
{

public Boolean call(String s) { return s.contains("b"); }

}).count();

System.out.println("Lines with x: " + nAs + ", lines with y: " +
nBs);

}
}
```

Chapter 3- Batch Processing in Spark

Before beginning to learn the complex tasks of the batch processing in Spark, you need to know how to operate the Spark shell. However, for those who are used to using the Python or the Scala shell, then the better as you can skip this step.

Begin by launching the Scala console. This can be done by typing the following command:

```
scala
```

We now need to declare a list having some integers, and this will be given the name "ourNumbers." The following command can be used for doing this:

```
scala> val ourNumbers = List(3, 2, 5, 9, 1, 7)
ourNumbers: List[Int] = List(3, 2, 5, 9, 1, 7)
```

We now need to declare a function which will be used to compute the cube of a particular integer. This can be done as shown below:

```
scala> def cube(x: Int): Int = x * x * x
cube: (x: Int)Int
```

The function has been given the name "cube."

We should then use the map function so as to apply the function which we have created to the numbers that we have. This can be done as shown below:

scala> ourNumbers.map(a => cube(a))

res: List[Int] = List(27, 8, 125, 729, 1, 343)

// there are shorthand ways on how this can be done in Scala.

// ourNumbers.map(cube(_))

// ourNumbers.map(cube)

You have now learned how to perform some operations on the shell. That is how simple it is for one to use.

How to use the Spark shell

With Spark, once one has run the Spark shell, the app ID should be specified, which is connected to the Spark cluster. The app ID will be similar to the application entry as shown in the web UI under the applications which are running. If you just begin by performing a download of a dataset for the purpose of experimentation. The spam dataset can be obtained by running the following command:

Wget http://www.stat.stanford.edu/~tibs/ElemStatLearn/datasets/spam.data

It should then be loaded into a textfile in Spark by running the following command on the Spark shell:

```
scala> val inFile = sc.textFile("./spam.data")
```

With the above command, the file "spam.data" will be loaded into the Spark and each of the lines in the file will be contained in a separate entry of the RDD.

For those who have already been connected to the Spark master, the file might be loaded on one of the machines which are available on the cluster. This is why you should ensure that the file is made available on all of the machines in the cluster. If you need to make this file available on all of the machines, the following command can be used for executing the addFile function which will perform this:

```scala
scala> import spark.SparkFiles;

scala> val f = sc.addFile("spam.data")

scala> val iFile = sc.textFile(SparkFiles.get("spam.data"))
```

Note that with the Spark shell, the command history can easily be accessed. The up arrows can be pressed, and the previous commands will be shown. If you do not want to keep on typing each command until it is complete, just press the Tab key and it will be autocompleted. This is also applicable when you are not sure of how to write a particular command. To do a conversion to a useful format, then use the following command:

```scala
scala> val numbers = inFile.map(a => a.split(' ').map(_.toDouble))
```

Exploring Data by use of Spark

You might need to perform some statics on your data. Begin by starting the Spark shell as shown below:

Python:

```
/root/spark/pyspark
```

Scala:

```
/root/spark/spark-shell
```

After a few seconds, you will get the prompt. If you need to clear the log output, just hit the "Enter" key and all will be well.

The next step should be for us to create a RDD named "pagecounts" from the input files which we have. The SparkContext has already been created, and this is the sc. In Scala, this can be done as follows:

scala> sc

res: spark.SparkContext = spark.SparkContext@490d1h30

scala> val pagecounts = sc.textFile("/wiki/pagecounts")

In Python, execute the following commands so as to do this:

```
sc
<pyspark.context.SparkContext object at 0r45h5670783350>

>>> pagecounts =  sc.textFile("/wiki/pagecounts")
```

For you to obtain a specific number of records, you can use the operation "take," which belongs to the RDD. Consider the example given below:

```
scala> pagecounts.take(5)
```

The above command will give the first five records that you have. The command can be used on both Scala and in Python, and it will execute effectively. However, the result will be in the form of an array and in Scala, the elements will be separated by a comma. This is why the output will not be very readable. To make it more readable, we can traverse the array so that each element in the array is printed on its own line. The following command can be used for that purpose in Scala:

```
scala> pagecounts.take(5).foreach(println)
```

For Python users, then use the following command for this purpose:

```
>>> for a in pagecounts.take(5):
...   print a
```

Sometimes, you might need to know the number of records that are contained in your data set. The following command can be used for this purpose:

For Scala users, the command should be as follows:

```
scala> pagecounts.count
```

The same command should also be n used in Python. However, note that the command will execute for a while, so try to read ahead as the command runs. You will note that the console log will inform you of all of the tasks that will be carried out.

The process of reading from the disk each time we perform an operation on the RDD is a bit tiresome. To avoid this, we have to cache the RDD into the memory. Our Spark will start to shine from this point. The process can be done as follows:

In Scala:

```
scala> val cPages = pagecounts.filter(_.split(" ")(1) == "en").cache
```

In Python, this can be done as follows:

```
>>> cPages = pagecounts.filter(lambda a: a.split(" ")[1] == "en").cache()
```

Note that once the above command has been executed on the Spark shell, the RDD will be defined by Spark. However, no computation will be done due to the lazy computation. On the next time when any action has been applied on the cpages, the data will cached in the memory and across the slaves which are contained in your cluster. Two to three minutes will be enough for the Spark to scan your entire data set and you will finally have your results back. However, due to the effect of caching which we have just applied, the results should be returned a bit faster. For those who observe the console log very clean, they will realize that some lines will be available, and these will be an indication that some data was added to the cache.

To know the number of records that you have in your pages, just run the following command:

```
cPages.count
```

The command can be executed on both Scala and Python. Note that once the above command has been executed for the first time, it will take two to three minutes so as to execute. However, when you run it for the second time, you will realize that the command will run a bit faster. This is due to the effect of caching the data in the memory.

We need to do something a bit complex. Let us try to generate a histogram from the dataset that we have. If course, this should be in the range of some specified dates. A key value pair for each line should first be generated. The number of pageviews for the date should then be the date. For Scala users, begin by executing the following command:

```
scala> val cTuples = cPages.map(line  => line.split(" "))
```

The second command should be as follows:

```
scala>  val  cKeyValuePairs  =       cTuples.map(line  =>
(line(0).substring(0,  8), line(3).toInt))
```

For Python users, execute the following sequence of commands:

```
>>> cTuples = cPages.map(lambda a: a.split(" "))

    >>>  cKeyValuePairs  =  cTuples.map(lambda a:  (a[0][:8],
int(a[3])))
```

The next step should be shuffling of the data and grouping of all the values which have the same key together. The values for each key should then be finally summed together. For this pattern, a method named "reduceByKey" can be used for doing this conveniently. Use the command given below:

```
scala> cKeyValuePairs.reduceByKey(_+_, 1). Collect
```

The above example is for Scala users. For the users of Python, the command should be as follows:

```
cKeyValuePairs.reduceByKey(lambda  a, b: a + b, 1).collect()
```

With the collect method, the RDD which is the result will be converted into an array. A name for the result produced by the command should be created, otherwise, a default name for this will automatically be created. Our last three commands can be combined into a single command. In Scala, this will be as follows:

```
scala> cPages.map(line => line.split(" ")).map(line => (line(0).substring(0, 8), line(3).toInt)).reduceByKey(_+_, 1).collect
```

In Python, this should be as follows:

```
cPages.map(lambda a: a.split(" ")).map(lambda a: (a[0][:8], int(a[3]))).reduceByKey(lambda a, b: a + b, 1).collect()
```

Chapter 4- Spark on EC2

In the Spark's EC2 directory, there is the Spark-EC2 script which is used for launching, shutting down, and management of Spark clusters on the Amazon EC2. With this, the Spark, Shark, and HDFS will be automatically set up in your cluster and on your behalf. In case you have not created an EC2 account for yourself, then begin by creating one on Amazon.

First of all, an Amazon EC2 key pair will be needed, so create one. To do this, just login to your Amazon Web Services account by use of the AWS console, on the left sidebar, click on the "Key Pairs." You can then create and download your key. You also have to ensure that the permissions for the private key file are set to 600. This will mean that only reading and writing of it will be allowed, and you will be in a position to use ssh. For the script to be used, one has to change or set some parameters to what is necessary.

How to Launch a Cluster

Begin by navigating to the EC2 directory of the Spark which you have downloaded.

You can then run the following command from this directory:

./spark-ec2 -k <keypair> -i <key-file> -s <number-slaves> launch <name-of-cluster>

In the above command, the name of your EC2 pair is the "keypair," and this should be the name which you provided when you were creating it. The "key-file" here is the private key file indentifying your key pair. The "number-slave" is the number of the slave which is to be launched by the node. The parameter "name-of-cluster" signifies the name that you need to give to your cluster.

Once everything has been started, check to see if the cluster scheduler is up and whether it is seeing all the slaves by just opening the web UI, and this can be found at the end of the script. If you need to see more options for usage, then run the following command:

./spark-ec2 –help

The following are some of the options which can be printed:

instance-type=<INSTANCE_TYPE>- this is used when we want to specify the instance of EC2 that we need to use. At the moment, only 64-bit versions are supported by the script, and a default one is provided.

region=<EC2_REGION>- this is used for the specification of a region of EC2 in which the instance is to be launched.

zone=<EC2_ZONE>- this is used for specification of an EC2 availability zone in which the instances will be launched. Note that a single zone does not have enough capacity, so sometimes you might get an error. If this happens, try to launch the instance in another zone.

zone=<EC2_ZONE>- this is used for attaching an EBS volume having a given amount of space to each of the nodes so that one can have a persistent HDFS cluster.

spot-price=PRICE- this is used for launching the worker nodes as Spot instances.

How to Run Applications

For you to run the applications, follow the steps given below:

Begin by navigating to the EC2 directory where you have stored the Spark which you have downloaded.

We now need to ssh into the cluster. Just run the following command:

./spark-ec2 -k <keypair> -i <key-file> login <cluster-name>

The parameters "keypair" and "key-file" should not change since we mentioned what they are earlier.

For the purpose of deployment of data or code into the cluster, just login and then use the script "~/spark-ec2/copy-dir."

For those whose applications are in need of accessing large datasets and you need to do it faster, you can load it from the Amazon S3 or just from an Amazon EBS device and then into a Distributed File System of Hadoop on your nodes. An instance of the HDFS will be set for you by the Spark-EC2 script. The installation of this was done in the "/root/ephemeral-hdfs" and to access it, you can use the script "bin/hadoop" in the directory. Note that once you stop and then restart your machine, the data contained in the HDFS will go away.

The directory "/root/persistent-hdfs" has a persistent HDFS instance and this will be tasked with the keeping of data across cluster restarts. Note that each node in the cluster will have little space for persistent data but this can be altered so that the persistent data can be stored in each node.

Some of you might get errors while running their applications. If this happens, then look at the logs for the slaves inside the work directory for the scheduler. You can also use the web UI so as to view the status of your cluster.

For the purpose of configuration, the file "/root/spark/conf/spark-env.sh" which is located on each machine of the cluster can be edited so that the Spark configuration options like the JVM options can be set up. So that changes can be reflected in each of the machines, the file has to be copied to each of them. However, doing this manually can be a bit tiresome. There is the script "copy-dir" which can be used for this purpose, and the process will have been made easier. Begin by editing the file "spark-env.sh" located in the master, and then run the command "~/spark-ec2/copy-dir /root/spark/conf" which will RSYNC it to all of the workers.

You also need to know the data EC2 nodes cannot be recovered once they have been shut down. This is why you should first copy them before you can stop them. Just navigate to the EC2 directory of the Spark which you downloaded and then execute the following command:

./spark-ec2 destroy <cluster-name>

Pausing and Restarting of Clusters

With the Spark EC2, a cluster can easily be paused. When this happens, the VMs are stopped, but they are not terminated. All the data which is contained in the ephemeral disks will be lost, but it will be kept in the persistent HDFS and in the root partitions. The machines which have been stopped will not cost you any cycles for EC2, but money for EBS storage will be a cost.

If you need to stop a single cluster, navigate to the EC2 directory, and then execute the following command:

./spark-ec2 stop <cluster-name>

If you need to restart the cluster, then run the command given below:

./spark-ec2 -i <key-file> start <cluster-name>

You might also need to totally destroy the cluster so that it consumes no more EBS space. To do this, just run the following command:

./spark-ec2 destroy <cluster-name>

However, there are some limitations associated with the Spark on EC2. There is a limited support for cluster compute, and it provides no means for how a locality group can be specified. However, slave nodes can be launched in the <clusterName> manually, and then the Spark-EC2 launch –resume can be used for starting of the cluster.

How to Access Data in S3

The file interface of Spark makes it possible for it to process data in Amazon S3 by use of the same URI formats which are supported for Hadoop. In S3, a path can be specified as the input through the URI taking the form "s3n://<bucket>/path." The credentials for your Amazon security will also have to be provided. This can be done by setting the parameters AWS_SECRET_ACCESS_KEY and AWS_ACCESS_KEY_ID which are environmental variables, and these can be set before the program or through the SparkContext.hadoopConfiguration. If you need to learn all the instructions on how to access S3 by use of Hadoop, input libraries can be accessed in the Hadoop S3 page.

Chapter 5- Spark on GCE

GCE stands for Google Compute Engine. It is an infrastructure as a service which lets you execute your large scale computing workloads on the virtual machines which have been hosted at the infrastructure for Google. It is also possible for you to create your own and new machine and this will take you a very short time.

The following are the installation steps:

Begin by creating a CentOS image on the GCE. The space used should be at least 3.8 GB, otherwise the system will not compile.

Once you are done, you can perform an ssh into the new machine. An example of how this can be done is shown below:

gcloud compute --service_version="xyx1" --project="spark-project-1" ssh --zone="europe-west1-a" "spark-box-3g"

The next step should be the installation of Java. The following command can be used for this purpose:

sudo yum install java-1.7.0-openjdk-devel

To see the packages which are available for your download, just use the following command:

yum search java | grep 'java-'

You should also ensure that Python, Java, and Scala have been installed.

The next step should involve the installation of Git. This can be done by executing the command given below:

yum install git

You can then use the "wget" command so as to obtain the necessary packages online.

You can then run the assembly sbt/sbt.

Once you have completed the above steps, you will be done and set to go.

Chapter 6- Spark and Stand-Alone Clusters

Sometimes, you might need to install Spark in a standalone mode. In this case, a compiled version of Spark has to be placed on each node of the cluster.

How to Restart a Cluster Manually

If you need to manually start a standalone master serve, just execute the following command:

```
./sbin/start-master.sh
```

You will realize that after starting the master, a spark://HOST:PORT URL will be printed out and this can be used for the purpose of connecting the workers or for passing the arguments for the master to the SparkContext. This URL can also be found in the web UI for the master. The default URL for this is the one for the local host. At the same time, one can choose to start one or even more workers whom they can connect to the master.

It is after the worker has been started that one can look for the web UI of the master. The new node should be among the ones which are in the list, and the number of CPUs and the size of the memory will be shown. However, for the case of the memory, 1 gigabyte will be subtracted so that it can be used by the OS.

You should also pass the following parameters to both the worker and the master:

-i IP, --ip IP- this is the DNS name or the IP address which is to be listened to.

--webui-port PORT- this is the port for the web UI.

-p PORT, --port PORT- this is the port for which the service is to listen on.

-d DIR, --work-dir DIR- this is the directory to be used for the scratch space and the logs for the job output. This should only be for the worker.

-m MEM, --memory MEM- this is the total amount of memory for allowing Spark applications to be used on the machine, in the format like 1000M or 2G.

-c CORES, --cores CORES- these are the total CPU cores for allowing Spark applications to use on the machine and it should only be on the worker. The default setting is that it should be available for all.

Those are the parameters which should be passed.

Once the cluster has been set up, you should then connect your application to it. To do this, you just have to pass the spark://IP:PORT URL of the master to the constructor of the SparkContext. If you need to execute your Spark shell interactively against the cluster, just execute the following command:

./bin/spark-shell --master spark://IP:PORT

The option --cores <numCores> can also be passed to the command so as to control the number of cores the Spark shell will use in the cluster.

How to Launch the Compiled Spark Applications

The script spark-submit provides us with an effective and straightforward mechanism on how we can submit our Spark application to a cluster once it has been compiled. Inthe case of standalone clusters, installation of the driver inside the client process is currently supported by the Spark which is submitting the application. However, this is only possible in the client deploy mode.

Once an application has been launched via the Spark submit, the application jar will then be distributed to all of the worker nodes. If there are some additional jars that your application is using, then you should the flag –jars so as to specify them, and a comma should be used as a delimiter. The configuration or the execution environment of the application can also be specified.

Scheduling of Resources

The standalone cluster mode supports only a FIFO scheduler across the applications. However, you might need to involve multiple and concurrent users in the app. If this is the case, then one is encouraged to control the maximum number of resources that each of the applications will make use of. By default, the application will obtain all of the cores contained in the cluster, and this will be effective only when you run a single application at a time. The number of cores can be controlled by setting the spark.cores.max in the file SparkConf. An example of this is given below:

```
val con = new SparkConf()
.setMaster(...)
.setAppName(...)
.set("spark.cores.max", "10")
val sc = new SparkContext(conf)
```

Also, the parameter spark.deploy.defaultCores can also be configured on the cluster master process so that the default settings for the application can be changed and the setting which does not set the parameter spark.cores.max to something which is less than infinite. To do this, open the file "conf/spark-env.sh" and then add the following line of code to it:

```
Export SPARK_MASTER_OPTS="-
Dspark.deploy.defaultCores=<value>"
```

The above feature is very useful in the case of shared clusters and in which the users may have not configured the maximum number of cores on their individual machines.

Logging and Monitoring

With the standalone mode of Spark, a web based user interface is provided, which enables us to effectively monitor the cluster. The worker and the master are provided with their own web UI which is responsible for the showing of job statistics and the cluster. The default setting is that the web UI for the master can be accessed at the port 8080. However, one can choose to change this port, and this can be done either via the command line options or via the configuration file.

In the directory "SPARK_HOME/work," one can find a detailed output log for each of the jobs which is executed. Two files for each of the jobs will be provided, that is, stderr and stdout and all the output which was written to the console will be provided here.

Running Spark Alongside Hadoop

Spark can be used alongside a Hadoop cluster which is in existence, and this can be done by launching it as a separate service in your machines. For those who want to access the data for Hadoop but from Spark, just use the hdfs:// URL, but the right URL for doing this can be found from the Namenode URL for Hadoop. A separate cluster for the Spark can also be set, and it will also be in a position to access the HDFS via the network. However, this will take much time compared to accessing the local disk, but for those who are running on the same local network, this may not be a concern to them.

You need to know that with Spark, a heavy use of the network will be involved. In some environments, there might be very strict requirements regarding the use of tight firewall settings. There are some ports which you have to configure for this purpose.

In the case of standalone scheduling clusters, these are prone to failures. However, for the purpose of decision-making, the scheduler will use a master. This leads to creation of a single point of failure because in case the master fails to work or crashes, then we will be unable to create new applications. However, in order to solve this problem, there are two schemes on how the availability can be ensured.

Local File Recovery for Single-Node Recovery

With ZooKeeper, the availability in a production environment can easily be ensured. For those who only need to be in a position to restart the master once it goes down, then there is another way how this can easily be done. After the registration of both workers and applications, they will be having an enough state written to the directory which has been provided so that once the master process has been restarted, then these will be recovered.

For the purpose of enabling the recovery mode, the parameter SPARK_DAEMON_JAVA_OPTS can be set by use of the configurations given below:

spark.deploy.recoveryMode- this property should be set to FILESYSTEM so that the mode for single-recovery can be enabled. The default setting for this is none.

spark.deploy.recoveryDirectory- this should be the directory in which the recovery state for Spark will be stored. This will be accessible from the perspective of the Master.

Standby Masters with ZooKeeper

This involves making use of ZooKeer so as to perform an election of the leader and a state of storage. With this, multiple masters can be launched in the master which is connected to the instance of ZooKeeper. Once one of them has been elected to be the leader, the rest will be kept in the standby mode. In case the acting leader dies, then another master will have to be elected so that it becomes the leader.

The process of scheduling will then be resumed. Note that the process of recovery should only take between one and two minutes, and this should be from the time that the first leader went down. The delay will only affect the process of scheduling of new applications, and the applications which were in the state of execution during the time of failure of the master will not be affected in any way.

For this mode of recovery to be enabled, the parameter SPARK_DAEMON_JAVA_OPTS should be set to the following configuration:

spark.deploy.recoveryMode- this property should be set to ZooKeeper for the standby Recovery Mode to be enabled. The default setting for this is NONE.

spark.deploy.zookeeper.url- this property specifies the ZooKeeper cluster URL.

spark.deploy.zookeeper.dir- this specifies the directory in the ZooKeeper which should be used for storage of the state for recovery.

Note that for those who might be having multiple masters in the cluster, in case you fail to perform the correct configuration so that masters can use the ZooKeeper, then they will not be in a position to discover each other correctly, and then each will think that it is a leader. This will mean that the state of the cluster will not be a healthy one. The reason is that each of the masters will be scheduled independently.

Once the ZooKeeper cluster has been set up, the process of enabling the high availability will be very easy and straightforward. What you need to do is to start multiple master processes on the different nodes which you have, but the ZooKeeper configuration in all of these nodes will be the same. Feel free to add or remove the masters at any time that you want.

For new applications to be scheduled or for workers to be added to the cluster, the IP address which identifies the node acting as the leader currently should be well known. For you to accomplish this, just pass in a list of the masters where the passing of a single one was done. This will force the SparkContext to begin the registration with both of the masters. This will mean that in case the first host does, the configuration will be okay since a new leader, which will be host two will be found.

However, it will be good for you to know the difference between the normal operation and registration with the master. When an application is in the process of being started or launched, it should find the node which is acting as the current leader, and then perform a registration with it. In case this leader fails or dies, then all of the applications which were previously registered will be contacted together with the workers, and they will be notified of a change in the leadership. This means that they will be notified of the new master during startup.

Chapter 7- Streaming in Spark

Spark streaming is a feature which provides us with a fault tolerant, and highly scalable streaming process.

Setting up the system

In this section, you will learn how to set up the system ready for streaming in both Scala and Java. For Scala users, this should be as follows:

* scala/sbt: This is the directory containing the SBT tools.

* scala/build.sbt: this is the project file for SBT.

* scala/Section.scala: this is the Main Scala program that that is to be used for editing, compiling and running.

* scala/Helper.scala: This is the scala file which has the helper functions for Section.scala

For Java users, this should be as follows:

* java/sbt: this is the directory having the SBT tool

* java/build.sbt: this is the project file for SBT

* java/Section.java this is the main program to edit, compile and run

* java/Heler.java: this is a java file which has few helper functions

* java/ScalaHelper.java: this is a Scala file which has few helper functions

We now need to have a look at the main file which is to be edited, compiled, and then run. This is the Section.java or the Section. Scala file. Its code is given below:

For Scala, it is as follows:

import spark._

import StreamingContext._

import spark.streaming._

import TutorialHelper._

object Section {

def main(args: Array[String]) {

// The Location of our Spark directory

val spHome = "/root/spark"

// The URL for the Spark cluster

val spUrl = getSparkUrl()

// where the JAR files are located

val jFile = "target/scala-2.9.3/section_2.9.3-0.1-SNAPSHOT.jar"

```
//Our HDFS directory for checkpointing purpose

val chpointDir =  Helper.getHdfsUrl() + "/checkpoint/"

// use twitter.txt for configuring the credentials of Twitter

}
}
```

For Java, this should be as follows:

```
import java.util.Arrays;

import spark.api.java.function.*;

import spark.api.java.*;

import scala.Tuple2;

import spark.streaming.*;

import spark.streaming.api.java.*;

import twitter4j.*;

public class Section {

public static void main(String[] args)  throws Exception {

//The Location of our Spark directory

String spHome = "/root/spark";

//The URL for the Spark cluster

String spUrl =  Helper.getSparkUrl();
```

```
//The Location having the required JAR files

String     jFile     =     "target/scala-     2.9.3/section_2.9.3-0.1-
SNAPSHOT.jar";

// The HDFS directory for purpose of checkpointing

String chpointDir =  Helper.getHdfsUrl() + "/checkpoint/";

// The login.txt text for twitter credentials

// The code should be added here

}
}
```

Note the use of the helper functions in the code which will help in adding the parameters which are needed for our exercises. The function "getSparkUrl()" will help in fetching the Spark cluster URL which is contained in the file "/root/spark-ec2/cluster-url."The function "configureTwitterCredential()" is also a helper function, and it will help in the configuration of Twitter authentication details by use of the file "/root/streaming/twitter.txt."

We should also configure the OAuth authentication for our Twitter account. For you to do this, a consumer key+secret pair has to be set up by use of the Twitter account.

You should begin by creating a new and a temporary application. To do this, just click on the blue button labeled "Create a new application." The following window will appear:

Create an application

Application Details

Name: *

tathadas-test

Description: *

something something

Website: *

http://www.something.com

Callback URL:

Developer Rules Of The Road

You can then provide the details about the application which are needed in the above form. In the case of the name, it has to be unique. After creation of the project, you will be asked to confirm it. At the window for doing this, you will see the consumer key and the consumer secret which the system has generated for you. For you to generate the access token and the access token secret, just navigate to the bottom and then click on the blue button labeled "Create my access token." You need to know that a confirmation will be available at the top which will tell you that it has been generated.

Your access token

It looks like you haven't authorized
token here, so you can start signing

Create my access token

If you need to obtain the keys and the secrets which are required for the purpose of authentication, click on the tab labeled "OAuth Tool" at the menu located at the top of the page. A page with all of the details will be presented to you.

You can then open the text editor of your choice so as to edit the configuration details of the Twitter. This is shown below:

cd /root/streaming/
vim twitter.txt

After execution of the above commands, the following template will be observed:

consumerKey =
consumerSecret =
accessToken =
accessTokenSecret =

The above should then be filled with the appropriate keys. These can be copied from the previous web page, and then pasted in the appropriate fields. Once you are done, it is good for you to perform a double check so as to ensure that the right keys have been provided in the right fields. You can then save your configuration settings before proceeding to write the program for streaming purpose.

Now, we want to write our program for streaming purpose. This should print the tweets that it receives each second. First, begin by opening the file with a text editor as shown below:

In Scala:

cd /root/streaming/scala/
vim Section.scala

In Java, this will be as follows:

```
cd /root/streaming/java/
vim Section.java
```

The following should be the next part for Scala users:

```
val tts = ssc.twitterStream()
```
For Java users, the above should be as follows:

```
JavaDStream<Status> tts = ssc.twitterStream();
```

To print some of the tweets which are available, let's go as follows:
Scala:

```
JavaDStream<Status> tts = ssc.twitterStream();
```

For Java, this will be as follows:

```
JavaDStream<String> st = tts.map(

new Function<Status, String>() {

public String call(Status st) { return st.getText(); }

}

);

st.print();
```

In the case of the intermediate data, we have to set some checkpointing operation. This can be done as follows:

Scala:

ssc.checkpoint(chpointDir)

Java:

ssc.checkpoint(chpointDir);

Our final step should be to inform the context to start the computation which we have just created. This can be done as follows:

Scala:

ssc.start()

Java:

ssc.start();

That is how the process can be done.

Conclusion

It can be concluded that Spark is an application which is used in cloud computing. The framework is used for speeding up the processing of analytical operations so that these can be increased even 100 times faster as compared to the other technologies which are in use today. The process of performing an interaction with data is usually associated with much complexity. With Spark, this complexity is greatly reduced, and the speed of processing is in turn improved at large.

The framework is also known for its wide support in different platforms, and this explains why it is liked by so many people compared to other frameworks which can be used for performing the same task. Since the release of the framework for the first time, it has been greatly improved and numerous changes have been implemented in it. This sawit developed into a top level project in the year 2014.

This expansion is still ongoing, and this shows how promising the framework might be in the future. The framework is also suitable for writing algorithms which are effective for use in machine learning. For one to use Spark, a distributed storage and a cluster manager are needed. This book is intended to help you on how to use Spark for performing of some analytics.